Foods

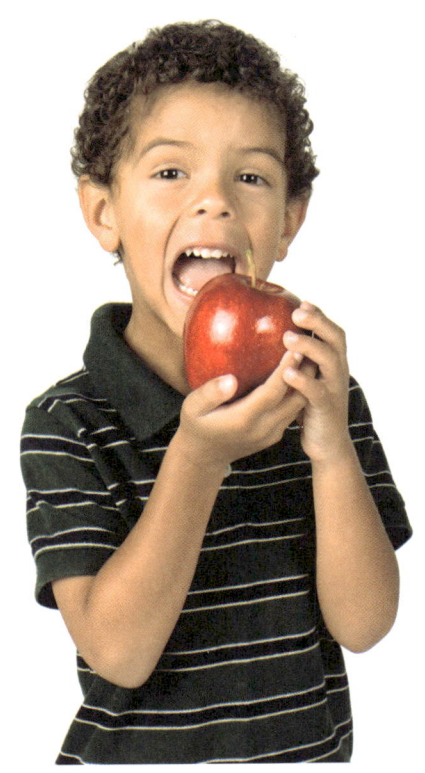

Seed Learning

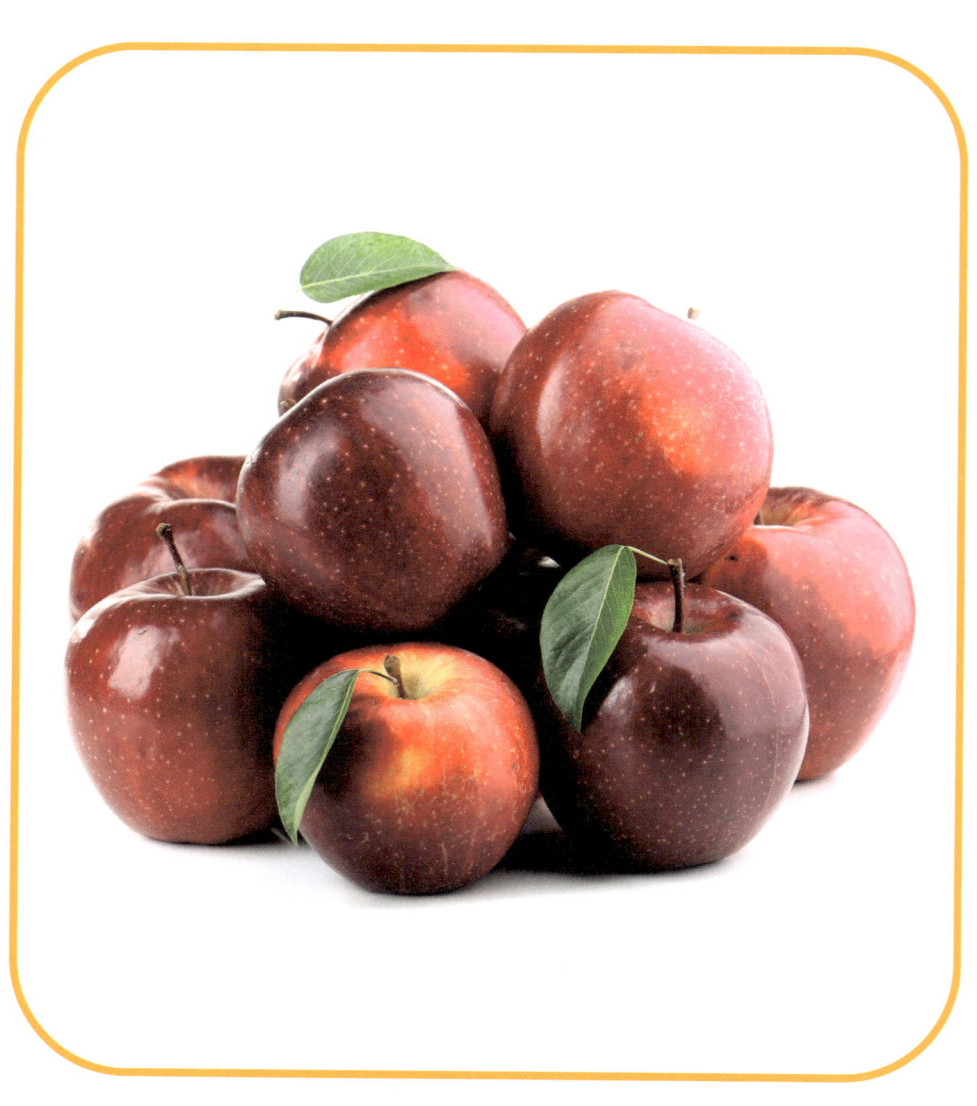

apples

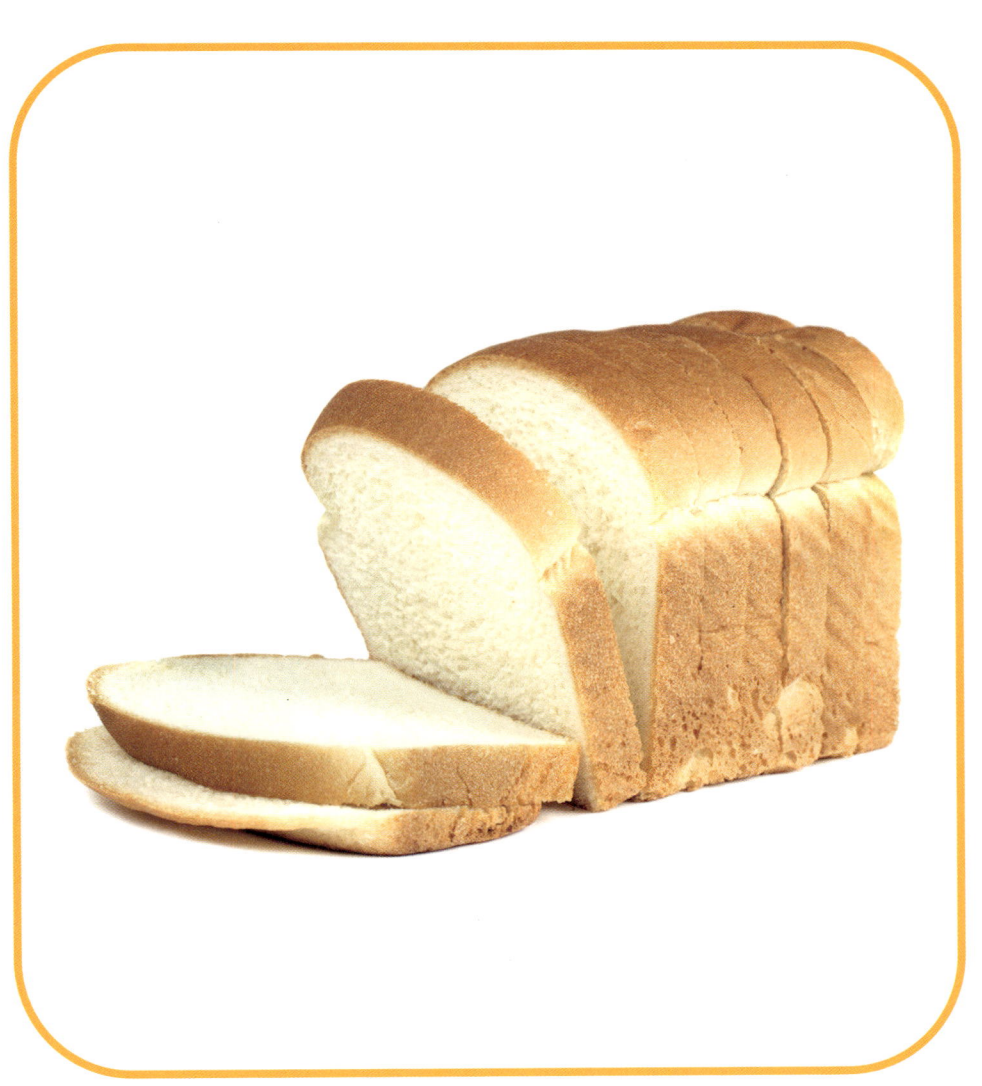

bread

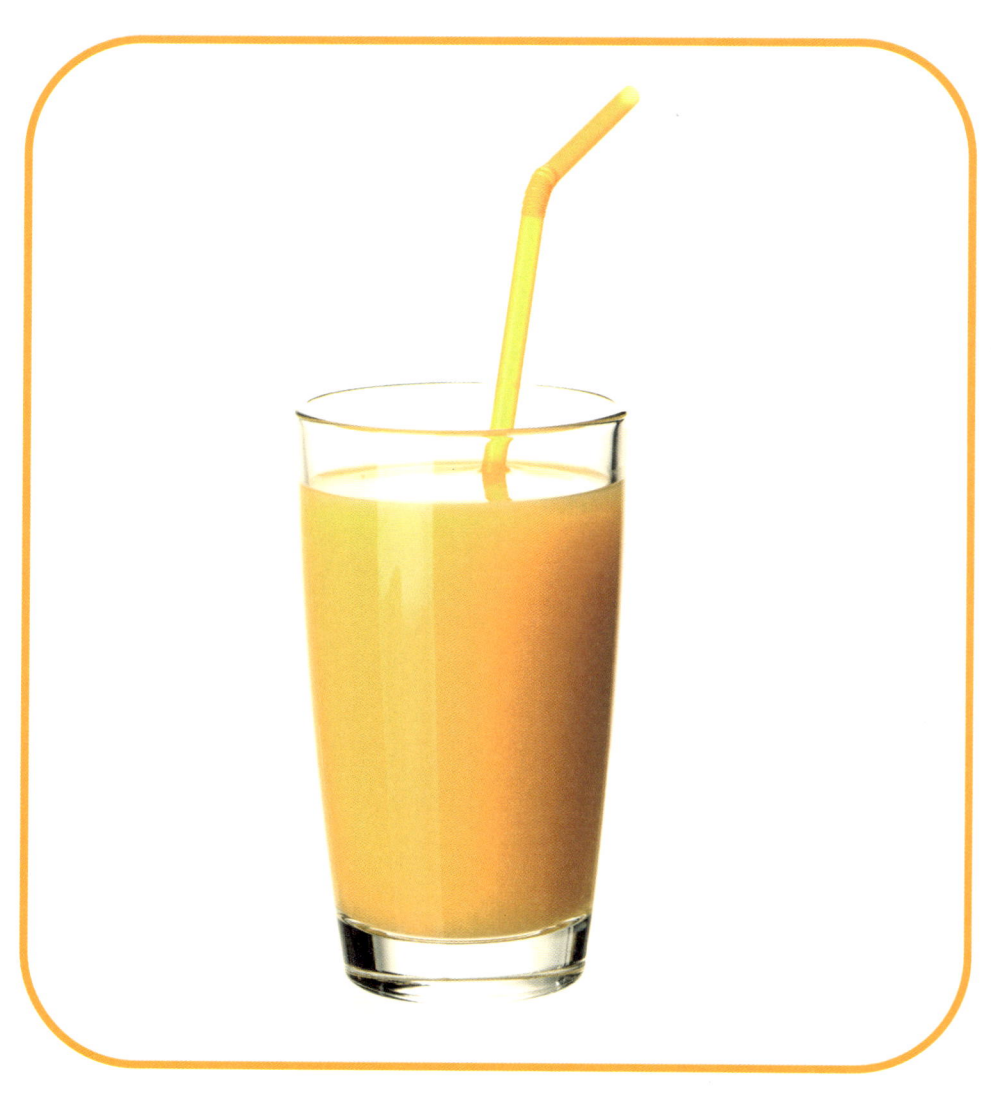

juice

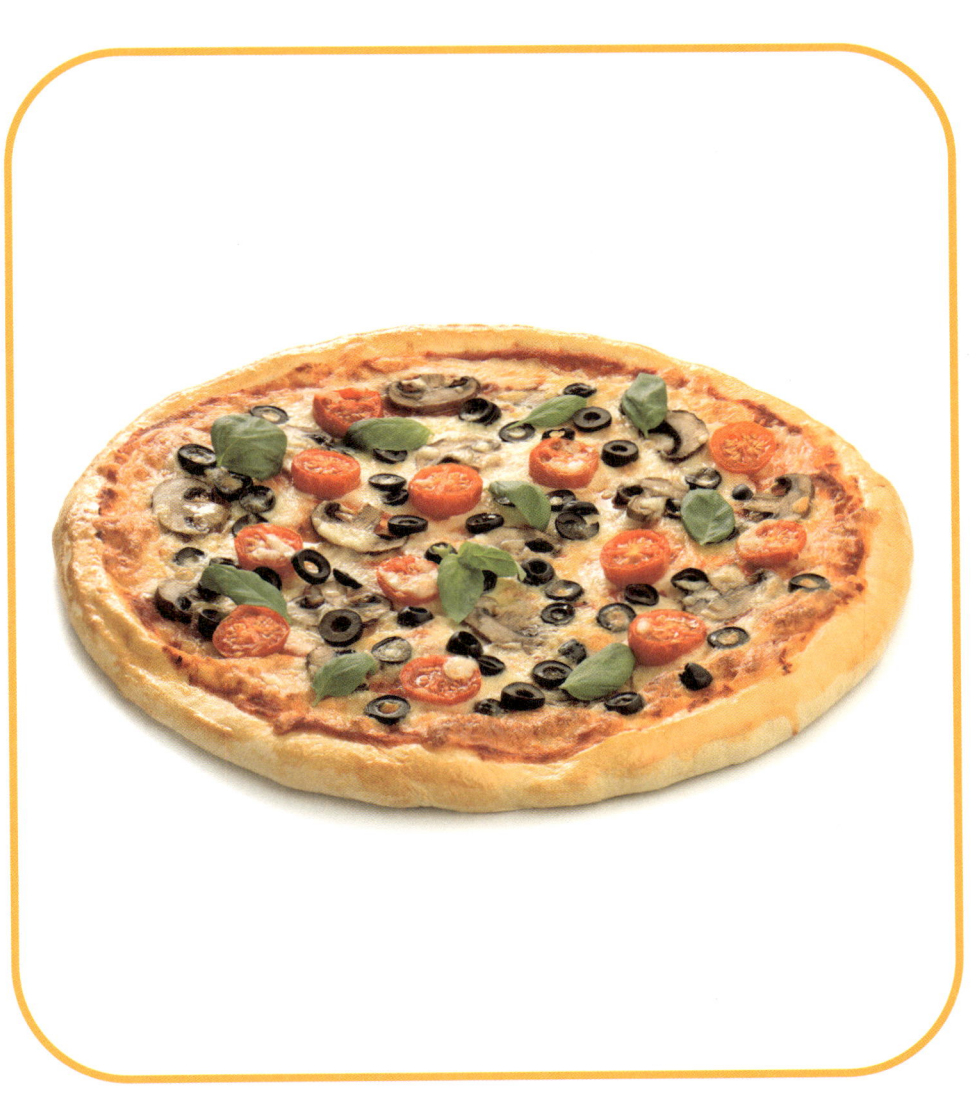

pizza

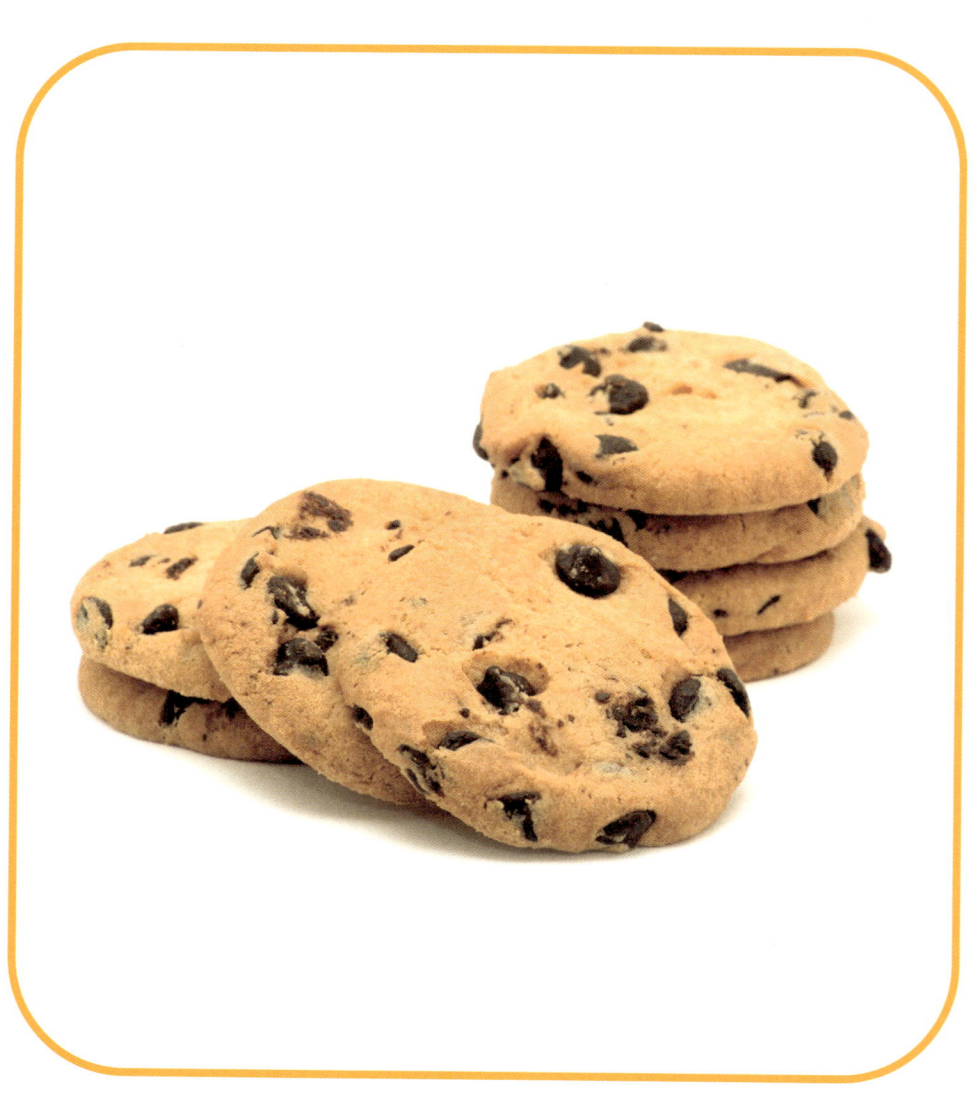

cookies

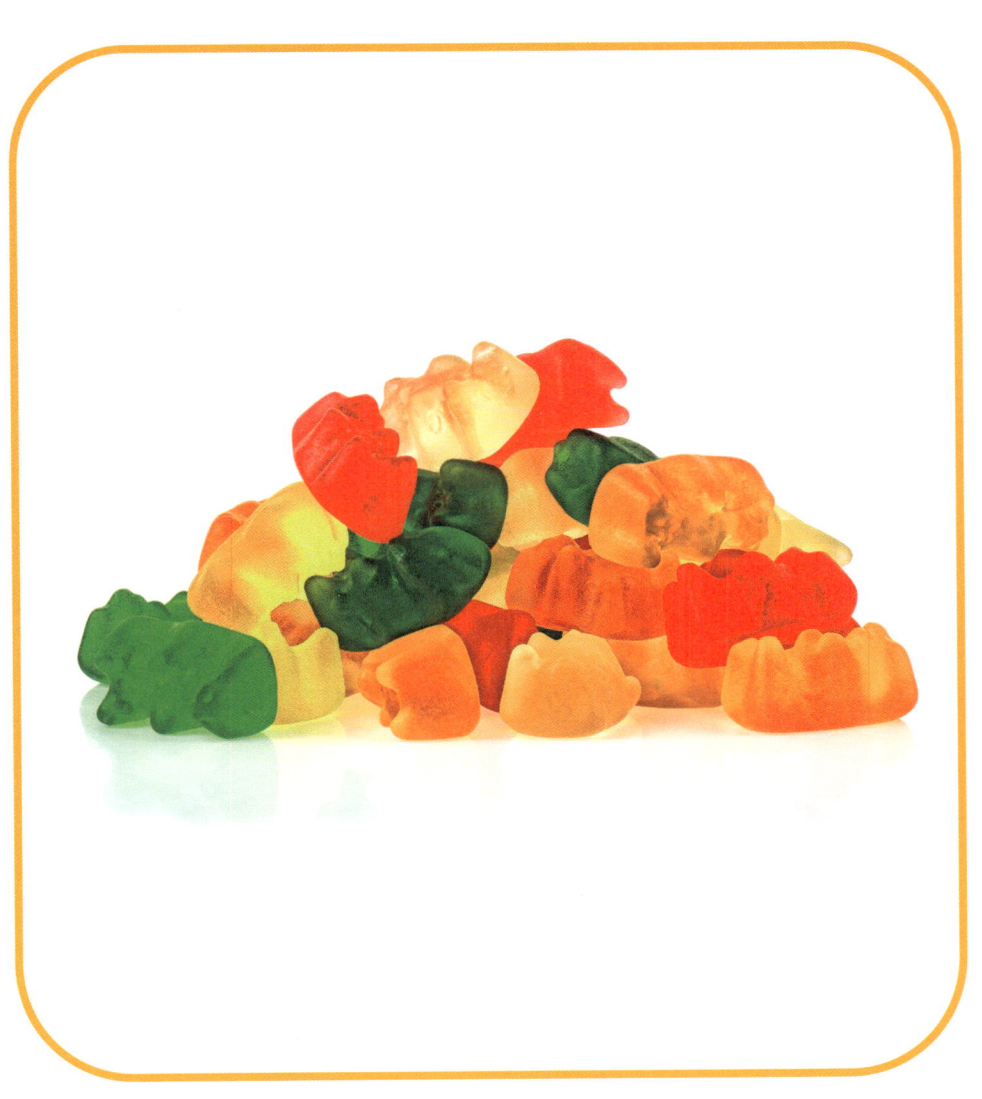

jelly

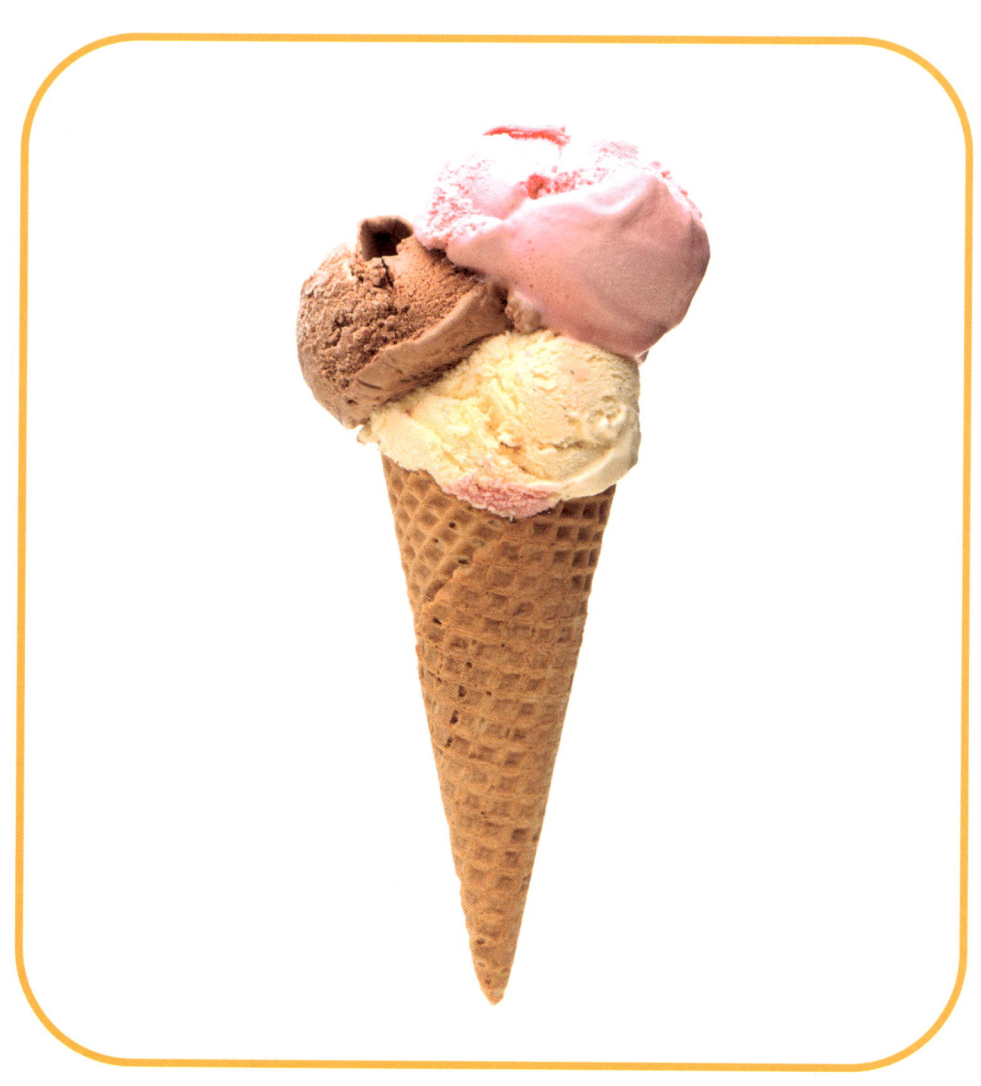

ice cream

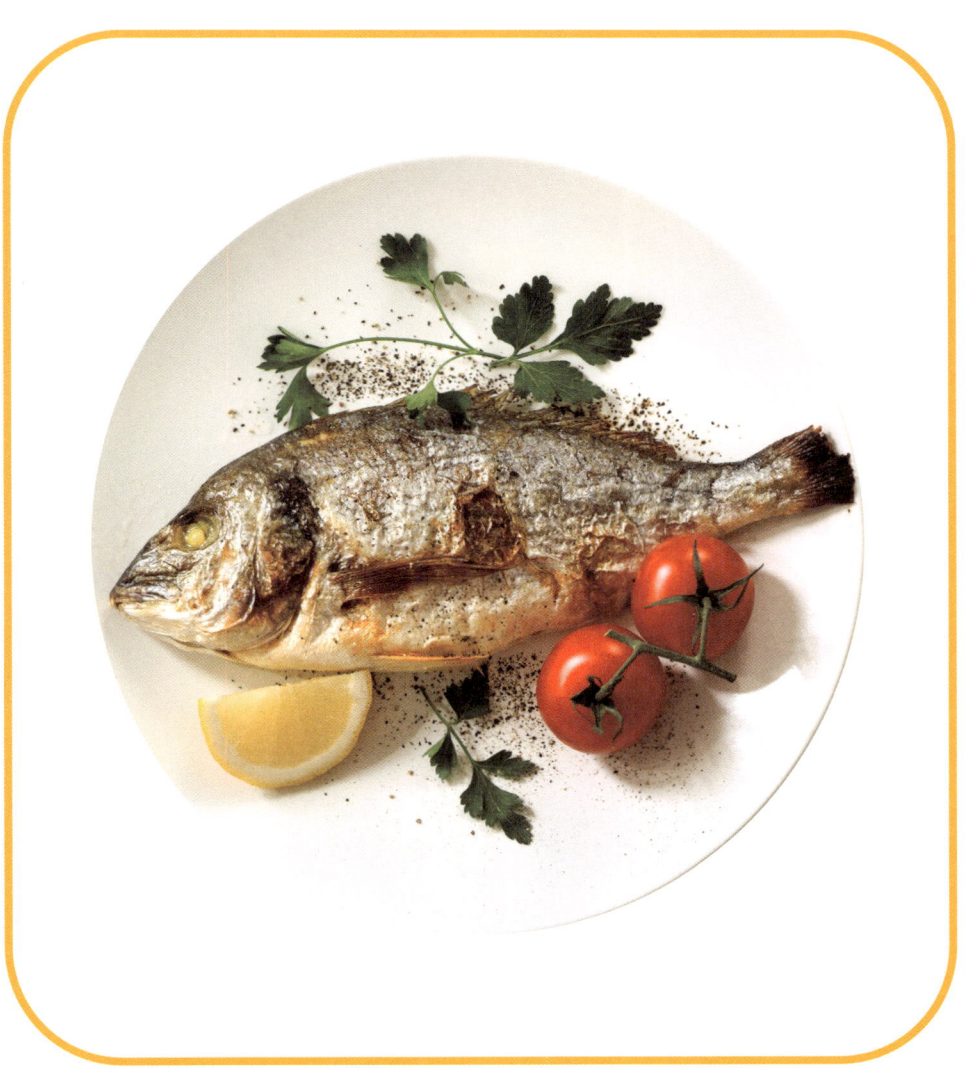

fish

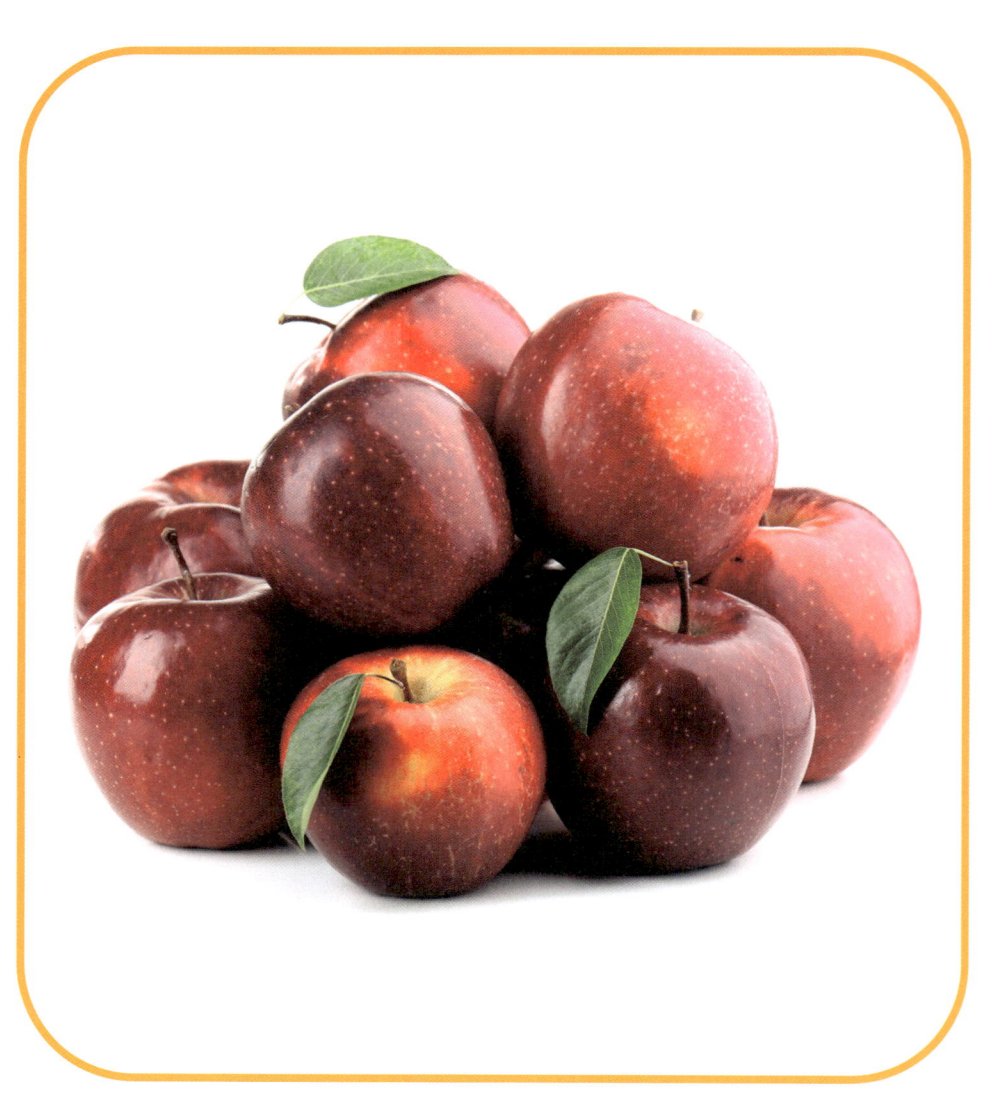

Do you like
apples?

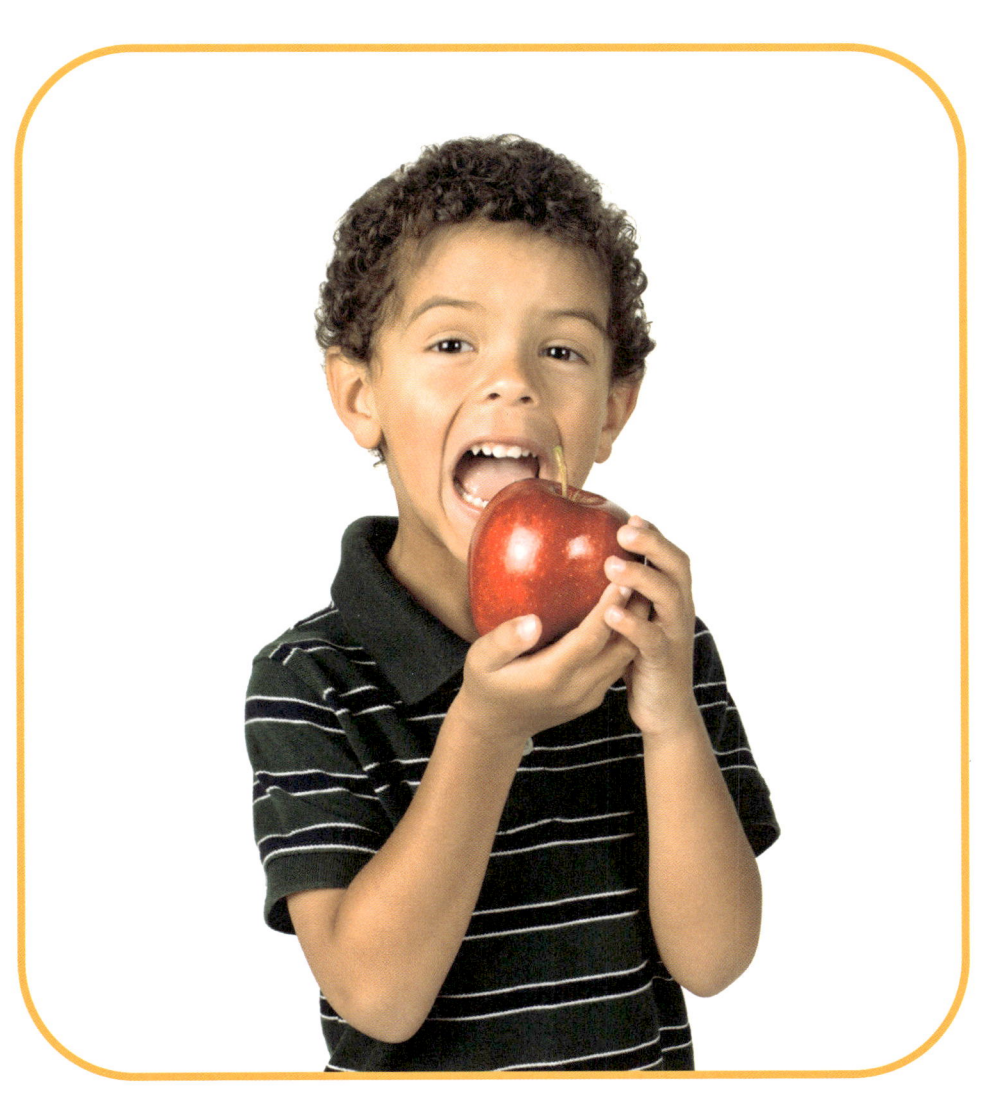

Yes, I do.

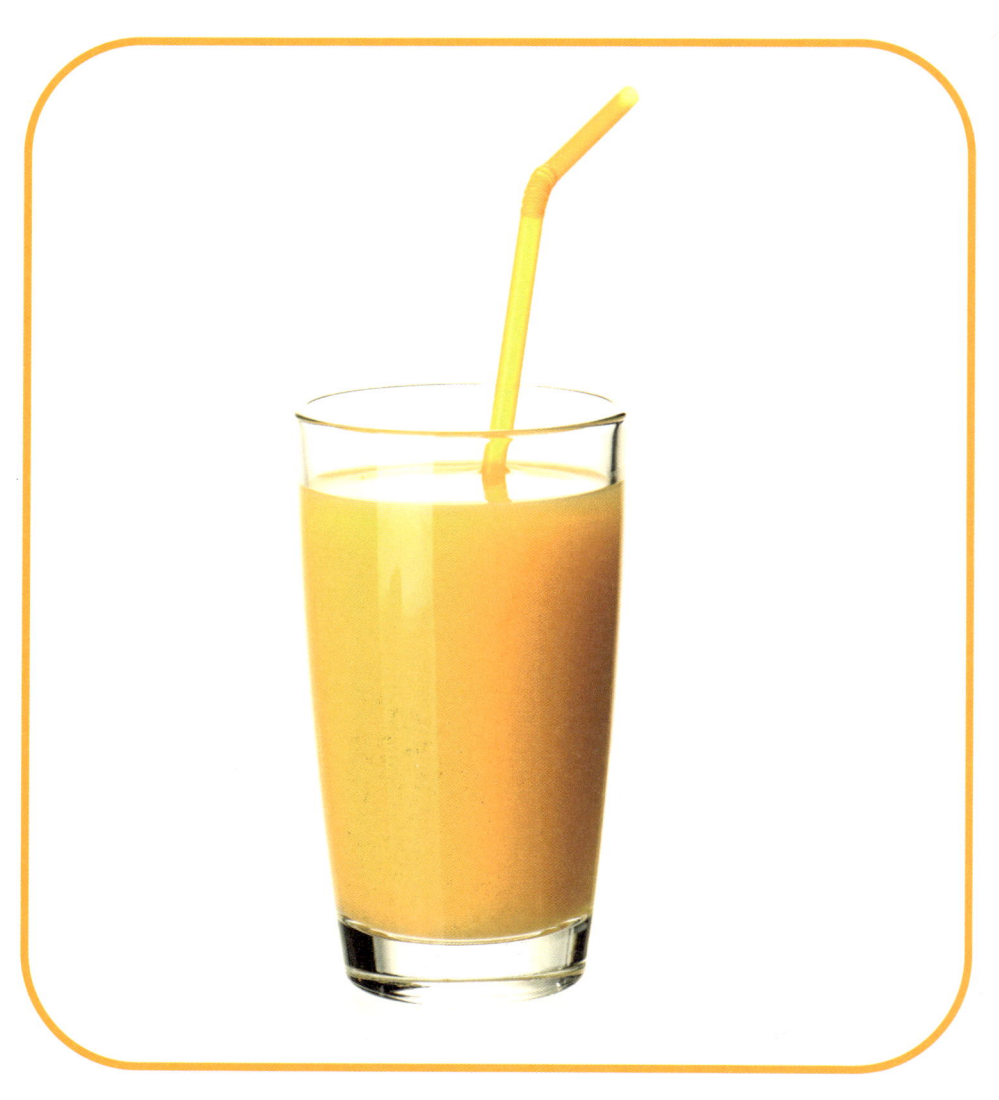

Do you like juice?

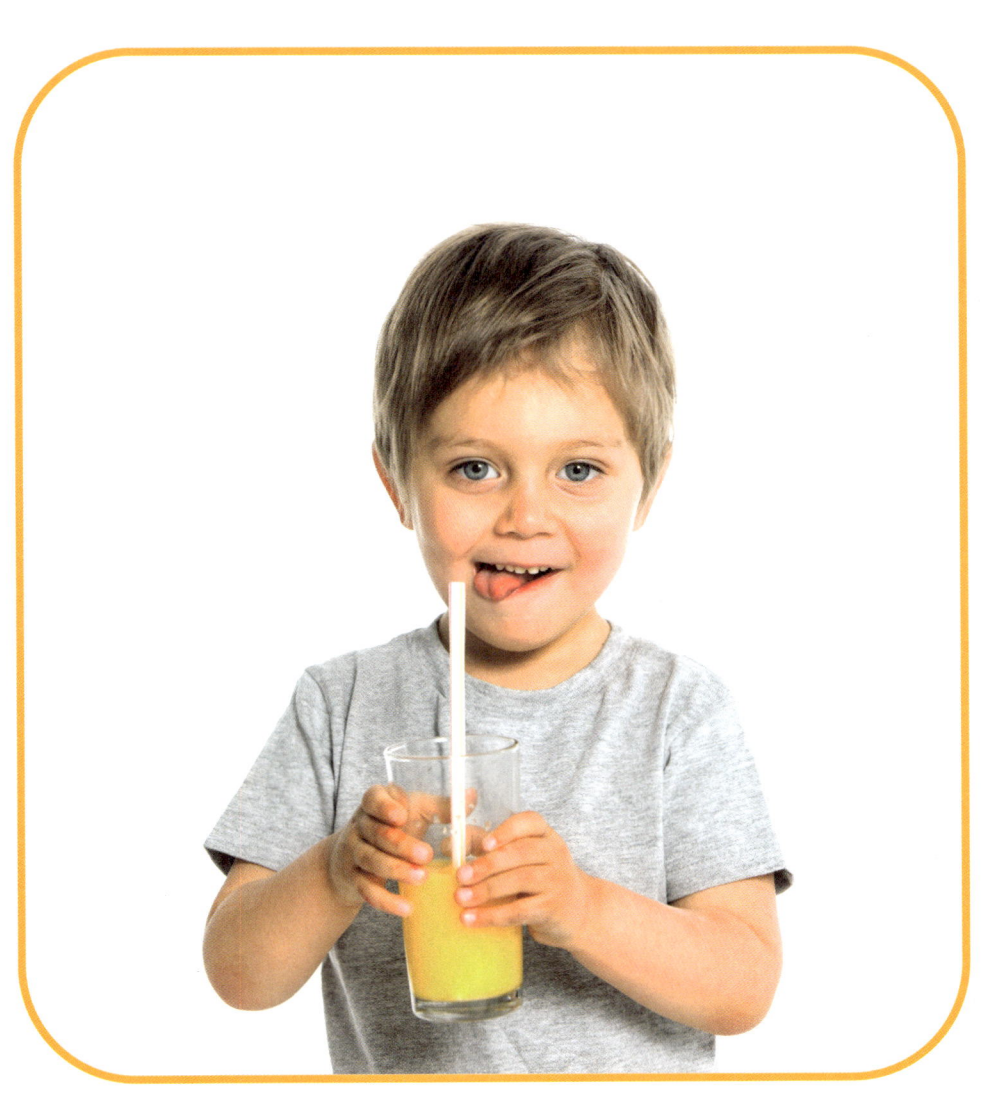

Yes, I do.

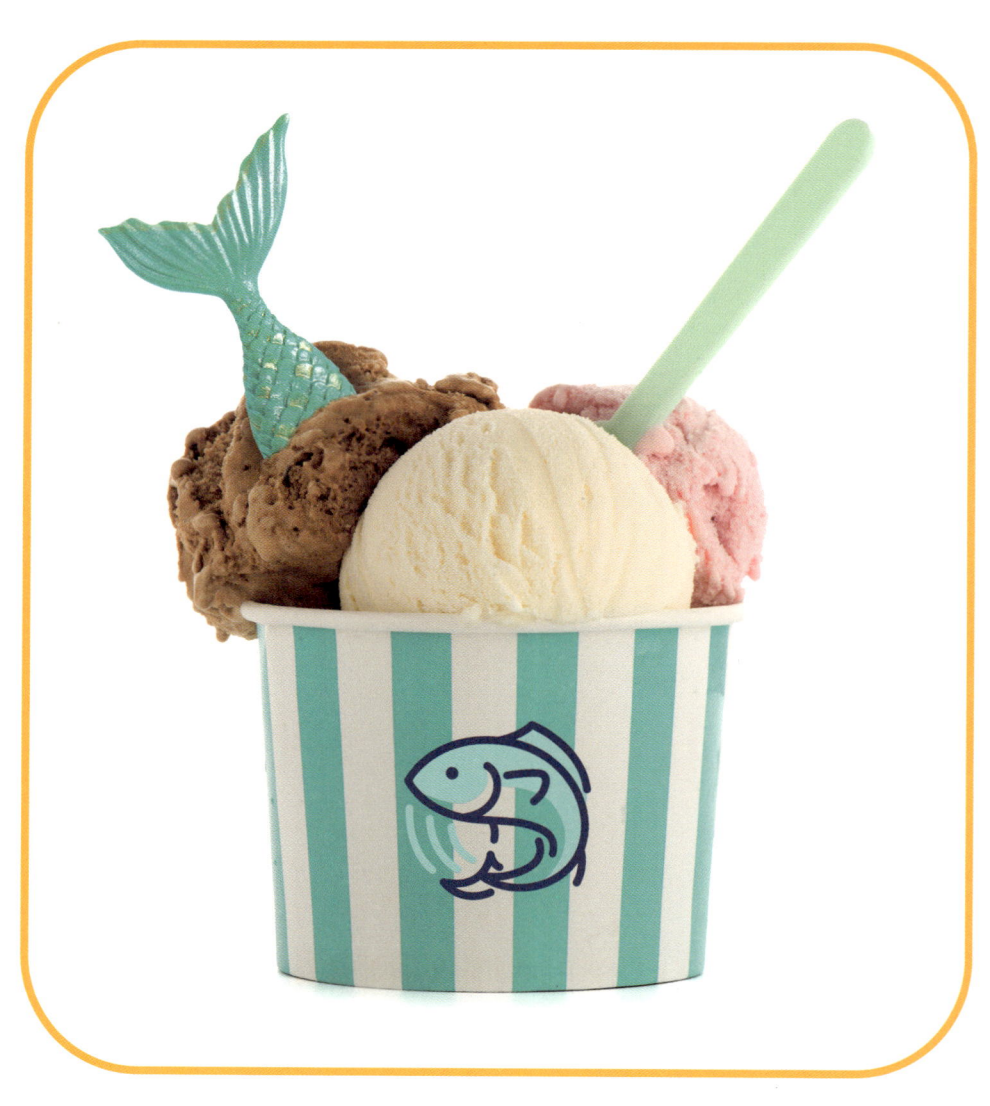

Do you like fish ice cream?

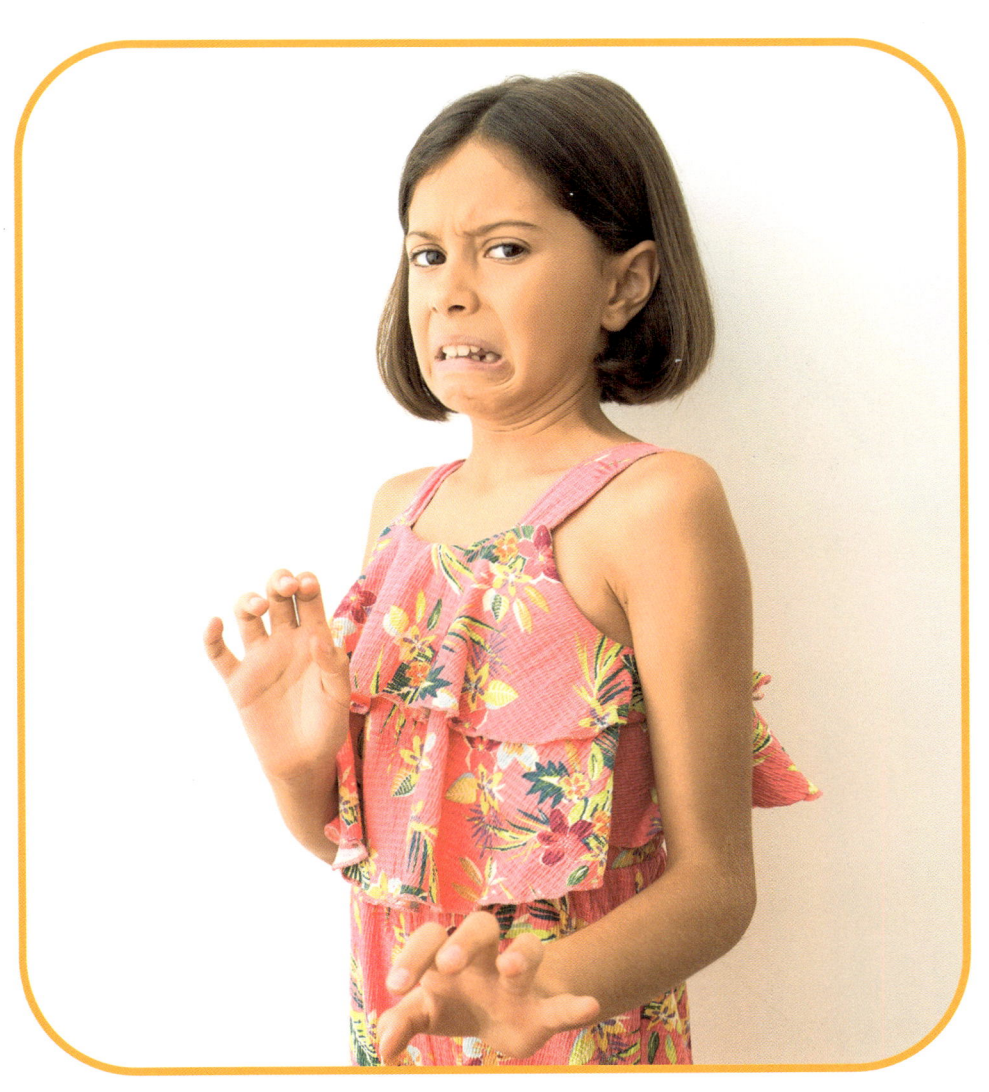

No, I don't.
Yuck!

Word List

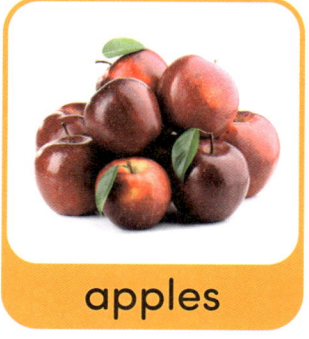

apples

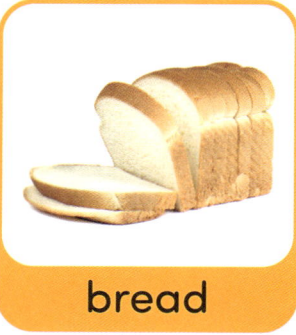

bread

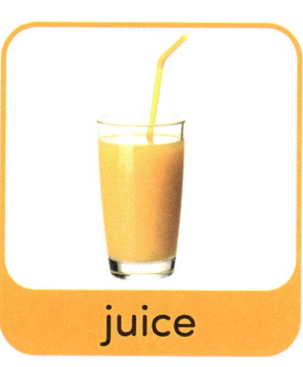

juice

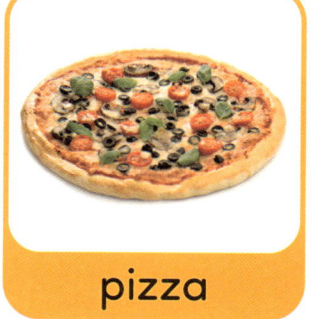

pizza

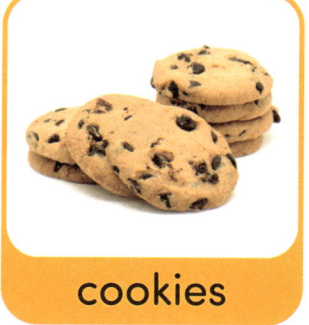

cookies

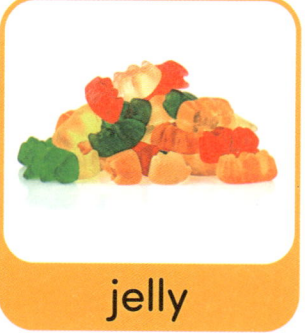

jelly

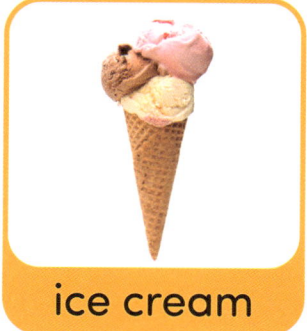

ice cream

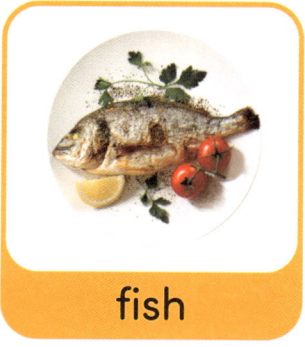

fish